On the Farm

Sheep
Ewes, Rams, and Lambs

Lorijo Metz

PowerKiDS press
New York

To David Watson, a veterinarian who, like a good shepherd, takes care of his flock

Published in 2011 by The Rosen Publishing Group, Inc.
29 East 21st Street, New York, NY 10010

First Edition

Editor: Amelie von Zumbusch
Book Design: Greg Tucker
Photo Researcher: Jessica Gerweck

Photo Credits: Cover, pp. 5, 7 (top), 8, 9, 10, 12, 14, 16, 17, 18, 22 Shutterstock.com; p. 4 Karl Weatherly/ Getty Images; p. 6 Reinhard Dirscherl/Visual Unlimited, Inc./Getty Images; p. 7 (bottom) Peter Moorman/Getty Images; p. 11 © www.iStockphoto.com/Leslie Morris; p. 13 Nick Koudis/Getty Images; p. 15 © www.iStockphoto. com/Stephen Patterson; p. 19 (top) Gale Zucker/Getty Images; p. 19 (bottom) © www.iStockphoto.com/Meredith Barcham; p. 20 © www.iStockphoto.com/Lisa Nguyen; p. 21 © Giulio Andreini/age fotostock.

Library of Congress Cataloging-in-Publication Data

Metz, Lorijo.
  Sheep : ewes, rams, and lambs / Lorijo Metz. — 1st ed.
    p. cm. — (On the farm)
  Includes index.
  ISBN 978-1-4488-0690-4 (library binding) — ISBN 978-1-4488-1341-4 (pbk.) —
ISBN 978-1-4488-1342-1 (6-pack)
  1. Sheep—Juvenile literature. I. Title. II. Series: Metz, Lorijo. On the farm.
  SF375.2.M48 2011
  636.3—dc22

                                    2010004853

Manufactured in the United States of America

CPSIA Compliance Information: Batch #WS10PK: For Further Information contact Rosen Publishing, New York, New York at 1-800-237-9932

Contents

Sheep in Our World

Do you ever pull on a wool sweater on a snowy day? Wool clothing keeps you warm, even when it gets wet. As you may know, wool comes from sheep.

Scientists think that sheep were the first farm animals to be **domesticated**. People have raised sheep for wool, meat, and milk for over 10,000 years!

This woman is feeding sheep on a farm in Sequim Washington. There are more than five million sheep on U.S. farms.

You can see the thick, warm wool on this sheep. Sheep wool is more elastic, or stretchy, than the hair or fur of most other animals is.

In the 1400s, Queen Isabella of Spain used money earned from sales of wool to pay for the **explorer** Christopher Columbus's trip to the New World. In 1773, explorer James Cook brought sheep to New Zealand. Today the country has more than 40 million sheep. That is almost 12 sheep for each person who lives there!

This flock, or group, of sheep lives on New Zealand's South Island.

Breeds of Sheep

Domesticated sheep are **descended** from the mouflon and urial. These are wild sheep from Asia. There are many kinds of wild sheep around the world. For example, the Rocky Mountain

These mouflon live in Austria. Mouflon were brought to several Mediterranean islands thousands of years ago and later to central Europe.

bighorn sheep lives in North America's Rocky Mountains.

There are more than 1,000 **breeds** of domesticated sheep. Some sheep are raised only for their wool, milk, or meat.

These animals are Romney sheep. Romney sheep are raised for both their meat and their wool.

People have bred other sheep to be useful for more than one purpose. Ossimi sheep, from Egypt, are raised for meat. They also produce **coarse** wool used for making rugs. The fat-tailed Karakul is one of the oldest breeds of domesticated sheep. It is good for wool, meat, and milk.

Kerry Hill sheep, such as those shown here, come from Powys, in the United Kingdom. They are known for their soft wool.

What Do Sheep Look Like?

White sheep are most common, but there are also lots of black sheep.

Sheep come in many colors, such as black, white, and even red. Some sheep have coats of more than one color. A few are even spotted.

Most sheep are born with tails. Farmers often dock, or cut off, sheep's tails. They do this to keep the sheep clean and make them easier to **shear**. Many breeds of sheep have horns. Others

Farm Facts

Male sheep are called rams and female sheep are called ewes. Baby sheep are called lambs.

Both male and female sheep can have horns. However, horns are more common on male sheep, such as this ram.

are polled, or have no horns. While two horns are common, some sheep, such as Najavo-churro sheep, can have four horns. Still others, such as Awassi sheep, can have up to six horns!

Follow the Sheep

Sheep live in groups, called flocks. Sheep flocks generally stay together while **grazing**. They also stay together for safety. When faced with a **predator**, such as a coyote, sheep run rather than fight. Their **instinct** to follow makes it easy to herd, or round up, large numbers of them. It also means that if one sheep heads into danger, others will follow.

As you can see in this picture, a flock of sheep generally stays close together when it travels across land.

A sheep's sharp senses of smell, hearing, and sight help it keep watch for predators, such as wolves.

Sheep have excellent eyesight. Their eyes are on the sides of their heads. This lets them see well on each side of them and behind them but not very well in front of them. Sheep also have excellent hearing. They can smell predators from far away, too.

The sheep in a flock recognize, or know, each other. Sheep remember the faces of other sheep.

Shepherds and Sheepdogs

Shepherds are people who take care of sheep. While sheep graze, shepherds watch over them. They make sure the sheep are safe from predators. In winter, shepherds

This guardian sheepdog is an Akbash dog. Akbash dogs come from Turkey. As many sheepdogs are, Akbash dogs are big and white.

make sure sheep have **shelter** from wind and plenty of food and water.

Border collies, such as this dog, are among the best-known and most skilled herding dogs. They are generally considered to be the smartest breed of dog.

Sheepdogs are a shepherd's best friends. Herding sheepdogs, such as the Border collie, herd sheep. A well-trained dog can herd a large flock of sheep and make them go just about anywhere. Other dogs, such as the Great Pyrenees and the Anatolian shepherd, are guardian sheepdogs. These dogs keep sheep safe from predators, such as wolves and mountain lions.

Little Lambs

As many young animals are, lambs are interested in the world around them. They have a lot to learn.

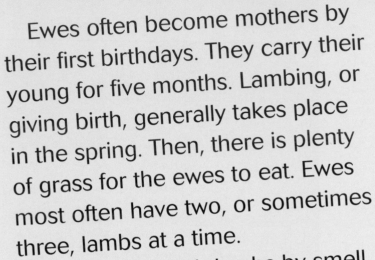

Ewes often become mothers by their first birthdays. They carry their young for five months. Lambing, or giving birth, generally takes place in the spring. Then, there is plenty of grass for the ewes to eat. Ewes most often have two, or sometimes three, lambs at a time.

Ewes know their lambs by smell. On some farms, mothers and lambs spend the first few days in a small pen called a jug. This is known as

Farm Facts

You can tell a sheep's age by its teeth. As sheep age, their teeth spread and break. Sheep that have lost all their teeth are called gummers.

Lambs like to spend time with their mothers. Sometimes they even climb up on their mothers' backs.

jugging. It gives ewes and lambs time to bond. This is important because ewes will feed their lambs only if they remember them.

Feeding Time

Sheep will graze all day long. However, they do most of their eating in the early morning and late evening.

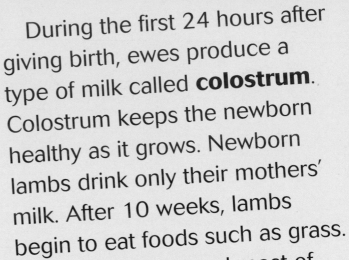

During the first 24 hours after giving birth, ewes produce a type of milk called **colostrum**. Colostrum keeps the newborn healthy as it grows. Newborn lambs drink only their mothers' milk. After 10 weeks, lambs begin to eat foods such as grass.

Adult sheep spend most of the day grazing. They eat grass, clover, and other plants. When there is no fresh grass, farmers

Farm Facts

Like cows and goats, sheep are ruminants. Ruminants are hoofed animals that have special four-part stomachs. These stomachs let them eat plants that need extra chewing.

These sheep are drinking water from a trough. Troughs are long, narrow things that hold food or water.

feed sheep hay, **silage**, and grains, such as corn and wheat. Farmers also give sheep plenty of clean water. They provide salt blocks for the sheep to lick, too. These supply sheep with important **nutrients**.

Soft, Warm Wool

Farmers generally shear sheep once a year. Shearing sheep does not hurt them. Just like hair, wool grows back. People trained to shear sheep can remove the **fleece** from a sheep in one piece in under 2 minutes!

This sheep is being sheared. You can see the thick fleece that is being cut off on the ground around the sheep.

Just as there are many breeds of sheep, there are many types of wool. Spinners are people who spin wool into yarn. They prize breeds, such as Romney sheep,

These people are knitting with wool. People often knit warm clothes, such as sweaters and scarves, out of wool.

with long, shiny wool. The coarse wool of Icelandic sheep is often used for making rugs. Things made from wool are warm, do not burn easily, and will last a long time.

This ewe and her lamb are merino sheep. Merino sheep first came from Spain. They are known for their fine wool.

Milk and Meat

Lamb is meat from sheep that are under one year old. Many Muslims and Christians eat lamb on important holidays. Mutton is meat from older sheep. Lots of Middle Eastern dishes, such as shish kebabs, may be made with mutton.

Comisana sheep, from Italy, and East Friesian sheep, from Germany, are common breeds

Dorper sheep, such as those shown here, are often raised for their meat. These sheep were first bred in South Africa.

of dairy sheep. Some people drink sheep's milk. However, farmers most often use it to make cheese. Feta is one cheese that is often made with sheep's milk. Greek spinach pie, called

This woman is making sheep's milk cheese in the Italian hamlet, or tiny village, of Vergelle. Vergelle is known for its excellent sheep's milk cheese.

spanakopita, uses feta. Italians use ricotta and pecorino Romano cheese in lasagna, one of their best-known dishes. Both of these cheeses are generally made from sheep's milk.

Lawn Mowers and Beyond

There are many uses for sheep. Raw wool has **lanolin** in it. Lanolin is used to make everything from tape to hand cream. Sheepskin makes fine leather. It is used to make gloves and boots.

These girls are holding their pet lambs. Today, people sometimes keep sheep as pets.

There is one use for sheep, however, that might surprise you. City officials in Turin, Italy, use sheep as lawn mowers! Every spring, shepherds lead 700 sheep into Turin. The sheep graze on the city parks for two months before returning to the mountains. Sheep are useful in so many ways!

Glossary

breeds (BREEDZ) Groups of animals that look alike and have the same relatives.

coarse (KAWRS) Not fine or smooth.

colostrum (kuh-LOS-trum) The special milk many mammal mothers make around the time their babies are born.

descended (dih-SEN-did) Born of a certain family or group.

domesticated (duh-MES-tih-kayt-id) Raised to live with people.

explorer (ek-SPLOR-er) A person who travels and looks for new land.

fleece (FLEES) The woolly coat of a sheep or other animal.

grazing (GRAYZ-ing) Feeding on grass.

instinct (IN-stinkt) The feeling every animal has that helps it know what to do.

lanolin (LA-nuh-lun) A kind of grease naturally found in wool.

nutrients (NOO-tree-unts) Food that a living thing needs to live and grow.

predator (PREH-duh-ter) An animal that kills other animals for food.

shear (SHEER) To shave the wool off a sheep.

shelter (SHEL-ter) A place that guards someone from weather or danger.

silage (SY-lij) A wet kind of feed for animals.

Index

A
Asia, 6

B
breeds, 6–8, 18, 20

C
Cook, James, 5

F
fleece, 18
flock(s), 10, 13

I
Isabella, Queen, 5

K
kinds, 6

L
lanolin, 22

M
meat, 4, 6–7, 20
milk, 4, 6–7, 16, 21
mouflon, 6

N
New World, 5
New Zealand, 5
nutrients, 17

P
people, 4–5, 7, 12, 18, 21
predator(s), 10–13

S
scientists, 4
shelter, 12
silage, 17
Spain, 5

U
urial, 6

W
wool, 4–7, 18–19, 22

Due to the changing nature of Internet links, PowerKids Press has developed an online list of Web sites related to the subject of this book. This site is updated regularly. Please use this link to access the list:
www.powerkidslinks.com/otf/sheep/